Jul[...]

We Lov[...]

Nana & Papa

Please read this daily it's
a wonderful book.

😊

"2018"

May You Be
Blessed with
All These Things

Blue Mountain Arts®

New and Best-Selling Titles

By Susan Polis Schutz:
To My Daughter with Love on the Important Things in Life
To My Son with Love

By Douglas Pagels:
For You, My Soul Mate
100 Things to Always Remember... and One Thing to Never Forget
Required Reading for All Teenagers

By Marci:
Friends Are Forever
10 Simple Things to Remember
To My Daughter
You Are My "Once in a Lifetime"

By Wally Amos, with Stu Glauberman:
The Path to Success Is Paved with Positive Thinking

By M. Butler and D. Mastromarino:
Take Time for You

By James Downton, Jr.:
Today, I Will... Words to Inspire Positive Life Changes

By Donna Fargo:
I Thanked God for You Today

Anthologies:
A Daughter Is Life's Greatest Gift
A Sister's Love Is Forever
A Son Is Life's Greatest Gift
Dream Big, Stay Positive, and Believe in Yourself
Friends for Life
God Is Always Watching Over You
Hang In There
Keep Believing in Yourself and Your Dreams
The Love Between a Mother and Daughter Is Forever
The Strength of Women
Think Positive Thoughts Every Day
Words Every Woman Should Remember

May You Be
Blessed with
All These Things

*Hopes and wishes
to keep in your
heart forever*

Douglas Pagels

Blue Mountain Press™
Boulder, Colorado

Library of Congress Control Number: 2012937791
ISBN: 978-1-59842-682-3

◧ and Blue Mountain Press are registered in U.S. Patent and Trademark Office.
Certain trademarks are used under license.

Printed in China.
Second Printing: 2013

✪ This book is printed on recycled paper.

This book is printed on paper that has been specially produced to be acid free (neutral pH) and contains no groundwood or unbleached pulp. It conforms with the requirements of the American National Standards Institute, Inc., so as to ensure that this book will last and be enjoyed by future generations.

Blue Mountain Arts, Inc.
P.O. Box 4549, Boulder, Colorado 80306

I hope you will remember all the hope and happiness that is wished for you through all the days ahead.

May the words in this book touch your heart, brighten your life, and bring you blessings that last forever...

May you be blessed with all these things

*A little more joy,
a little less stress,
a lot more understanding
of your wonderfulness.*

*Abundance in your life,
blessings in your days,
dreams that come true,
and hopes that stay.*

Friendship in many faces,
love in all its forms,
safe journeys, true success,
and sweet rewards.

Courage with its strength,
serenity with its calm,
the ability to always
hang in there and carry on.

A rainbow on the horizon,
an angel by your side,
and everything
that could ever bring
a smile to your life.

May you be blessed with a little more joy

May this book be like a packet of smiles for you... specially delivered from someone who would like to send a lasting gift of joy and encouragement your way!

May every one of your days be blessed with a sense of hope streaming in with the sunlight, a sense of strength woven into the winds, and as many things to be thankful for as there are stars in the sky.

I hope the distance between where you are and where you want to be grows shorter every day. May your journey through this world be touched by kindness, inspired by wisdom, graced with understanding, and kept as safe as possible from any harm.

I hope you have a charmed life and that every road ahead leads you to joys that are lasting and deep.

May you be blessed with
a little less stress

May the days be good to you:
comforting more often than crazy
and giving more often than taking.

May the passing seasons make sure
that any heartaches are replaced with
a thousand smiles and that any hard
journeys eventually turn into nice,
easy miles that take you
everywhere you want to go.

Remember that some of the secret joys of living are not found by rushing from point A to point B, but by slowing down and inventing some imaginary letters along the way.

These words will help you get through just about anything... Stay positive! (Hopeful people are happier people.) ← Choose wisely. (Good choices will come back to bless you.) ← Remember what matters. (The present moment. The good people in it. Hopes and dreams and feelings.)

← Don't stress out over things you can't control. (Just don't.) ← Count every blessing. (Even the little ones add up to a lot.) ← Be good to your body. (It's the only one you get.)

↶ Listen to the wishes of your heart. (It always seems to know what's true, what's right, what to do, and where to go with your life.)

↶ Understand how special you are! ↶ Realize how strong you can be. ↶ And know that, YES, you're going to make it through, no matter what.

Maybe you won't be dancing in the streets or jumping on the bed... but you are going to get through the day, the night, and each and every moment that lies ahead. (I promise.)

May you be blessed with a lot more understanding of your wonderfulness

I think it's true that people are a little bit like stars. There are millions of them to see, but there are always a few that shine brighter and more beautifully than all the others.

The people who warm your heart and bring you a smile... those are the kind you want your life to be blessed with. Those are the ones you just adore.

Of all the stars in the sky, you are one of the brightest. You are a very special light in lots of people's lives, and you are thanked for all the warmth and happiness you bring!

There are a few absolute gems in this world. They are the people who make a tremendous difference in other people's lives... with the smiles they give, the blessings they share, and the way they warm the hearts of everyone around them.

Those rare and remarkable people are so deserving of every hope and happiness. They are the people who are incredibly unique, enormously thanked, and endlessly appreciated for everything they do.

And one of those wonderful, deserving, and one-of-a-kind people is most definitely... you.

If it ever seems like you're getting overlooked and underappreciated, find reassurance and comfort in quietly saying this:

"I am aware that I am less than some people would prefer me to be, but most people are unaware that I am so much more than what they see."

Smile inside about all the good things you do! Even when no one else is singing your praises, feel free to sing all you want.

Your accomplishments — large or small, tremendous or tiny — help to make this world a better place.

*Y*ou are something — and someone — very special. You really are. No one else in this entire world is exactly like you, and there are so many marvelous things about you.

You are here to shine in your own wonderful way, sharing your smile in the best way you can and remembering all the while that a little light somewhere makes a brighter light everywhere.

You can — and you do — make an
invaluable contribution to this world. You
understand that your actions are capable
of turning anything around — and that
joys once lost can always be found again.

Never forget what a treasure you are.
That special person in the mirror may not
always get to hear all the compliments you
so sweetly deserve, but you are so worthy
of such an abundance... of friendship, joy,
and love.

May you be blessed with abundance in your life

Each day brings with it the miracle of a new beginning. Many of the moments ahead will be marvelously disguised as ordinary days, but each one of us has the chance to make something extraordinary out of them.

I want you to remember that the happiness you create today will remain forever in your memories. I want you to live by your own light and shine by your own star. I want you to do what you've always wanted to do with your life.

I want you to envision the gift that you are.

Someday... you'll see. It will all be worth it. All the hopes, all the dreams. The sacrifices. The courage. All the hard work. All of it will turn out to be abundantly worthwhile.

Someday you'll open the door on a brand-new day and be rewarded with everything working out just the way you wanted it to.

So never stop believing in the things you want to come true.

May you add a meaningful page to the diary of each new day. Do things that lift your spirits and help you rise above.

Walk along the pathways that lead to more happiness. And give your tomorrows what your yesterdays have only seen a glimpse of.

May you be given the gift of blessings in your days

May you count your blessings, one by one, and come up with a list that just makes you grin.

I want your life to be so rewarding! I wish you peace, deep within your soul, and joyfulness in the promise of each new day.

I wish you understanding of how special you truly are. I wish you a journey, safe from the storms and warmed by the sun.

I wish you friends, close at heart, even over the miles. I wish you loved ones — the best treasures we're given. And present moments to live in, one day at a time.

And I wish you new beginnings...
to give life a chance
to really shine.

I want you to be happy. I want you to fill your heart with feelings of wonder and inspiration. I want the world to treat you fairly, and I want the people you interact with on a daily basis to appreciate the remarkable person you are. I wish you the quiet, inner kind of contentment that comes around and warms your life with smiles deep inside. I know you'll be sure to make good choices on your journey through life, and I want you to be rewarded for those wise decisions.

I wish you the insight to see your inner and outer beauty. I wish you sweet dreams. I want you to have times when you feel like singing and dancing and laughing out loud. I want you to be able to make your good times better and your hard times easier to handle. I want you to have millions of moments when you find satisfaction in the things you do so wonderfully. And I wish I could find a way to tell you how important you are and how terrific you will always be.

May you be blessed with dreams that come true

I want you to keep planting the seeds of your dreams... because if you keep believing in them, they will keep trying their best to blossom for you.

It's encouraging to have a dream. It's something that gives so much more than it takes, always cheering you on and never holding you back.

It's empowering to have a dream. It's a steady source of inner strength for those who keep their hopes alive.

And it's so inspiring to have a dream. It's a reflection of the beauty of your soul and of who you are inside.

If you don't put limits on yourself, you can always keep striving. You might amaze yourself with what you discover you can do. If you want to reach out for happiness, don't ever forget that... you can go as far as your dreams can take you.

I hope your dreams take you...
to the corners of your smiles,
to the highest of your hopes,
to the windows of your opportunities,
and to the most special places
your heart has ever known.

Even if you can't change the world, never doubt that you can do remarkable things to change and rearrange your little corner of it.

Gardeners will tell you that the best time to plant a flower garden was years ago... and the second best time... is right now. The same philosophy that applies to flowers also holds true for personal goals. Just imagine this...

On this very day, even one year ago, if you had started a new goal, think how far along you would be! The best time to plant those seeds, follow those dreams, and start reaching for the sky... was back then.

The second best time to begin... is today.

Never let go of your dreams. There are things you would like to do in your life. There are dreams you wish would come true in your life. There are goals you want to reach, places you want to go, and things you hope to accomplish. There are people to meet, friends to make, and feelings of love you want to have in your heart.

There are so many wishes and desires that are a wonderful part of who you are.

Those things... are your dreams.

They're the things that fill your life with hope and happiness and that make your days rewarding and simply amazing.

Never let go of your dreams. Keep wanting them, working for them, and believing in them. Be strong and steady and devoted.

And never forget... on your journey through life, you will one day see... your accomplishments will far surpass any disappointments, your successes will triumph over any failures, and your dreams will bring you smiles and blessings and beautiful things... that you haven't even dreamed of yet.

May you be blessed with hopes that stay

None of us know what tomorrow will bring. But all of us can benefit from certain things we can do to see us through, no matter what.

Be open to new days, new ways, and new possibilities. Make the very best choices you can make. Learn from any challenges you face, grow from any difficulties, and go into the days ahead with the steady hope that things will be better. Because they will be.

Just hang in there and take everything one step at a time. Do all the positive things it takes to push any clouds away and help the sun shine through.

And remember... if you keep your faith strong and your hopes bright, one wonderful thing will happen in return...

They will always light the way for you.

*Hope can bring you peaceful moments
when the world around you is difficult
to comprehend.*

*Hope is a comforting reminder that
tomorrow will be here soon, ready to
give us a fresh, new start.*

*Hope is the warm and welcomed knowledge
that beautiful possibilities exist.*

*Hope is all these special things and —
in simply knowing this — when hope
is all you've got... you've still got a lot.*

Have hope. Be optimistic! And expect things to turn out for the best.

Remember that beyond the clouds, the sun is still shining. Meet each challenge and give it all you've got.

Count your blessings. Climb your ladders and have some nice, long talks with your wishing stars. Be strong and patient. Be gentle and wise. Do every positive thing you can possibly do.

And believe in happy endings... because you are the author of the story of your life.

May you be blessed with friendship in many faces

I wish you the closeness of others who can guide you, inspire you, comfort you, and light up your life with laughter. I want your life to overlap with the lives of those who understand your moods, who nurture your needs, and who lovingly know just what you're after.

I think it's one of the world's most wonderful blessings to have someone in your life who makes every day brighter, every hope stronger, every memory sweeter, every burden easier, and every season feel like it's the best one you've ever had.

A friend is one of the nicest things you can have and one of the best things you can be. A friend is a living treasure, and if you have one, you have one of the most valuable gifts in life.

A friend is the one who will always be beside you, through all the laughter and through each and every tear. A friend is a blessing you can always rely on; the someone you can always open up to; the one wonderful person who always believes in you in a way that no one else seems to.

A friend is a hand that is always holding yours, no matter where you are, no matter how close or far apart you may be. A friend is someone who is always there and will always — always — care. A friend is a feeling of forever in the heart.

A friend is the one door that is always open. A friend is the one to whom you can give your key. A friend is one of the nicest things you can have and one of the best things you can be.

*F*riendship is such a marvelous thing ← Friendship is two people who totally understand each other ← Friendship is so powerful ← It gives you support and strength to see your way through ← Friendship is a helping hand from someone with a very big heart ←

If there is a wall of worry in your life, a friend will help you get over it ← *Friendship is acceptance in its most beautiful form* ← *It is filled with grins and taking you in and giving you the kind of hugs that warm your whole world* ←

Friendship is a talking, listening, trusting thing ← *It reminds you that you don't have to keep everything bottled up inside* ← *It lets the genie out and helps so many wishes come true* ← *Friendship is the lovely reassurance of knowing that someone will always be there to check in on you* ← *Friendship is tons of fun, completely sweet, and enormously wonderful* ←

*I*n the dance of life, friends are the people who encourage you to be your best, who like you for who you are, who remind you what steps to take when you've forgotten the way, and who help you rest assured that your secrets are safe and your hopes are in good hands.

They help to balance things out, they keep you on your toes, they make you smile even when you're stumbling through life, and the stories, support, and laughter they bring to the years seem more like music to your ears than just about anything.

Good friends are one in a million.
Good friends are stories to share.
Good friends know the path to your
   happiness, and they walk with you
      all the way there.

Good friends are lives overlapping.
Good friends are laughter and tears.
Good friends are emotions so deep
   that the trust just keeps growing
      over the years.

Good friends are hard to find.
Good friends are easy to love.
Good friends are presents that
   last forever and that feel like
      gifts from above.

May you be given the gift of love in all its forms

Love is what holds everything together. It's the ribbon around the gift of life.

Love of family and love of friends... is where everything beautiful begins.

Ask me how important my family is to me and how essential my friends are, and I'll tell you this simple truth... nothing else even comes close.

The incredibly special connections we have with others are the things that matter most of all.

Whether they're close by or miles away, distance can never diminish what kindred souls feel in their hearts.

And whether time spent in each other's company is a little or a lot, every single moment is a present we're blessed with.

There is nothing more wonderful than telling the ones you cherish... how much they're loved and appreciated... every chance you get. There is no greater or more precious advice.

Love is what holds everything together. It's the ribbon around the gift of life.

*I*nside me there is a place... where my sweetest dreams reside, where my highest hopes are kept alive, where my deepest feelings are felt, and where my favorite memories are tucked away, safe and warm.

My heart is a lasting source of happiness. Only the most special things in my world get to come inside and stay there forever.

And every time I get in touch with the hopes, feelings, and memories in my life, I realize how deeply my heart has been touched... by love.

Love is amazing.

It brings you hope and joy. It warms your heart. As time goes by, it gets more comforting and grows even more understanding. It is soft and tender, but it is also tough and strong. It keeps you safe from any difficult or discouraging things going on in the world. It opens the door to wonderful possibilities that wouldn't exist any other way.

It lets you smile about the years to come. It brings a feeling of peace to your days. It gives you memories to treasure and so much to look forward to. And the more it shines in your heart, the more it will bless your life, over and over again.

"There is nothing more important than family."

Those seven words should be etched in stone on the sidewalks that lead to every happy home.

May you be blessed with a precious family... one that is filled with some of the best people you will ever know and one that inspires gratitude, joy, and deep appreciation.

Our families are such an essential part of our lives, our dreams, our highest hopes, and our sweetest memories.

When we have a caring family, we never have to worry about where we can go for a word of encouragement or who we can call on... just to talk about the day.

And we never have to wonder if the story of our life is going to turn out okay. We have a supporting cast of characters that love us (whether we deserve it or not), and we love them in return... no matter what. Like every life story, ours may have some ups and downs, but as long as a little bit of love shows up on every page... everything really is going to be okay.

If we're lucky in life, love comes to us in many forms. And if we're truly lucky... we get to feel that love every day... thanks to the blessing of a beautiful family.

What is love? Love is a wonderful gift. It's a present so precious words can barely begin to describe it. Love is a feeling, the deepest and sweetest of all. It's incredibly strong and amazingly gentle at the very same time. It is a blessing that should be counted every day. It is nourishment for the soul. It is devotion, constantly letting each person know how supportive its certainty can be. Love is a heart filled with affection for the most important person in your life. Love is looking at the special someone who makes your world go round and absolutely loving what you see.

Love gives meaning to one's world and magic to a million hopes and dreams. It makes the morning shine more brightly and each season seem like it's the nicest one anyone ever had.

Love is an invaluable bond that enriches every good thing in life. It gives each hug a tenderness, each heart a happiness, each spirit a steady lift.

Love is an invisible connection that is exquisitely felt by those who know the joy, feel the warmth, share the sweetness, and celebrate the gift.

May you be blessed with safe journeys

It's never too late to turn your life's journey into everything you want it to be. Have steppingstones to look forward to and milestones to look back upon, and as you continue on your way, enjoy this grand scheme of connect-the-dots days that lead the way to success and happiness.

As you travel toward the promises that lie ahead, I hope you have a safe journey on a smooth and steady path.

And as your future unfolds, I hope you will be inspired by all the people who have encouraged you in your lifetime, all the words that have touched your heart, and all the dreams you've ever wanted to come true. Let that inspiration join you on your journey, and let it be a guiding light that always shines for you.

Each day is like a room you spend time in before you move to the next. And in each room there is a door which leads to more serenity in life.

Leave behind the little worries. Tomorrow they won't matter, and next month you may not even remember what they were. Take the others one at a time, and you'll be amazed at how your difficulties manage to become easier to deal with.

Find your smile. Warm yourself with your quiet determination and your knowledge of brighter days ahead. Do the things that need to be done. Say the words that need to be said.

Happiness is waiting for you. Believe in your ability. Cross your bridges. Listen to your heart. Your faith in tomorrow will always help you do what is right, and it will help you be safe and strong along the path of life.

May you be blessed with true success

Success is so much more than most people imagine it to be. Success is looking forward to the day. It's having plans and wishes and goals to go after. It's letting your heart say yes.

Success is having fun and being healthy and finding ways to stay sane in this crazy world of ours. Success is dealing with the tears and minimizing any worries. It's cherishing your loved ones and hanging out with friends.

Being a success means doing a laundry list of things to make tomorrow brighter... for you and the people you're spinning around on this planet with...

Success is the reward you receive for all the good things you do. It's knowing, even as you work away all those hours of the day, you're setting the stage for something around the corner. Success is keeping the faith that you'll get where you want to go. It's staying the path when you need to, starting a new journey when you have to, and either way... continuing to discover more and more about the wonder of all this.

Success isn't just at the end of the rainbow. It's also found in the little things you do every day. So keep chasing your dreams and don't stop until you catch them.

And be sure to enjoy each blessing along the way.

May you be blessed with sweet rewards

For the times when you wonder how everything is going to work out...

You will eventually, proudly, happily discover that all the good things you can do — having the right attitude, having a strong belief in your abilities, making great choices and responsible decisions — all those things will pay huge dividends.

You'll see. Your prayers will be heard. Your karma will kick in. The sacrifices you make will be repaid. And the good work will have all been worth it.

*I wish you quiet times
all to yourself...
when the grace of all that
is good in your life is
sweetly celebrated within.*

Every day is a present we are given. Every sunrise comes along to shine in our lives, bring us new opportunities, and help us have a better understanding of who we can be and what we can achieve.

The best thing to do with the present... is untie the ribbons, discover the blessings, and make the most of everything the new day brings.

May you have times in your life that unfold with so many wonderful things... with doors that open on new beginnings, with windows that look out on a world filled with dreams waiting to come true, and with a sense of everything going in the direction you want it to.

May you be given the gift of courage... with its strength

In the days ahead, I know you will stay as strong as you need to be... to see your way through anything that comes along. I know that you will discover more courage and hope and faith inside you than you even knew you had.

I know that things will get better day by day and that the passage of time has a wonderful way of helping you see things in the right light.

And I know you can do every positive thing it takes to make it through any difficult time because that's what remarkable people do.

And one of those very special people, without a doubt... will always be you.

*T*here are times in life when just being brave is all you need to be.

We may not always know what to do next... or how to get where we're going in life, but if we just stay strong, trust in our faith, and make the very best choices we possibly can, a few things may not go as planned... but almost everything else will turn out right.

When you are in need of courage and strength, I encourage you to rely on all the good things that would love to make themselves available to you: inner peace, reaching out, steady goals, staying strong, and all your wonderful qualities that have always seen you through... and that will continue to carry you on.

May you be blessed with serenity... with its calm

Serenity is the reward for having the determination to make your life brighter and working, step by step, to get things right. It's relying on strength and courage and all the support you need to have a new and very special life. God's gift to every one of us is that we can mend and begin again and never give up. Serenity is the sun that follows the storm, and it's the warmth of knowing how good life can be.

*N*othing wastes more energy than worrying. The longer one carries a problem, the heavier it gets. Don't take things too seriously.

Live a life of serenity,
    not a life of regrets.

There have been times when I've found myself wondering... how am I going to make it through? What can I possibly do to remedy a certain problem? How am I ever going to figure out what direction to go in from here? And then I remember these words...

"When you must, you can."

That phrase has proven itself to be true in almost everything I've done. I've had days when I found strength inside me that I didn't even know I had. I found answers to problems I thought I'd never solve...

I have surprised myself with my ability to rise above certain situations and do what it takes to find my serenity. At times when I didn't think I could go on another day, I reached deep and kept the faith and managed to find a way.

It's something I plan on remembering as long as I live, and I hope it will bring its beautiful blessing... to you.

"When you must, you can."
    You can see your way through.

May you be blessed with the ability to always hang in there and carry on

Life... *it can be complicated.*

But when it is, I hope — with all my heart — that you find the answers you need to see you through.

I pray that any worries you're experiencing will turn out to be temporary problems and that they give way to permanent solutions and brighter days.

When life gets complicated, I think the best things we can do are these... being patient, staying strong, and remembering that "this too shall pass."

Life just gets crazy and complicated sometimes, and it would be nearly impossible not to get frazzled when it does. But don't ever forget... every morning is a new beginning and a fresh, new page in the diary of your life. Even though some of yesterday's story may have gone wrong...

I hope that soon... it will all go right.

I wish you all the best, every day, in every way.

And I wish you blue skies and sunshine, but I know that gray clouds can sometimes come along and stay around much longer than we'd like them to.

If life ever finds you going through a time like that, I hope you will always remember... that the sun is still shining above the clouds and it won't be long before it shines on you again.

I think that keeping a positive attitude helps immensely when you're in the process of seeing your way through. Life will always have its ups and downs, but don't ever forget: you are an incredibly capable person who can hang tough, hold on, and balance things out. Rely on your smile, reflect on your faith, go one step at a time, and just stay strong.

And do everything it takes to follow those wise and wonderful words:

"Keep calm... and carry on."

May you be blessed with a rainbow on the horizon

May the colors of your day be beautiful reflections of all these things...

Blue skies. Big smiles. Sweet dreams. Memories you'll treasure forever. Faith and courage to see you through. And reminders of how special you are.

Joy to give you twinkles in your eyes. Rainbows that rise above. Health and hope on this journey through life. And the very best... of everything!

Just remember that it's true...

It takes rain to make rainbows,
lemons to make lemonade,
and sometimes it takes
difficulties to make us
stronger and better people.

*S*ometimes it's important to work for that pot of gold. But other times it's essential to take time off and make sure that your most important decision in the day simply consists of choosing which color to slide down on the rainbow.

I want you to be truly happy.
To discover some more sweetness
within the days. To be given some
more serenity. To search out more
rainbows. To find some more time
that is yours to spend as wisely
and as wonderfully as you can.

May you be blessed with an angel by your side

May you always have an angel by your side ⬿ Watching out for you in all the things you do ⬿ Reminding you to keep believing in brighter days ⬿ Finding ways for your wishes and dreams to come true ⬿ Giving you hope that is as certain as the sun ⬿ Giving you the strength of serenity as your guide ⬿ May you always have love and comfort and courage ⬿

And may you always have an angel by your side ⟜ Someone there to catch you if you fall ⟜ Encouraging your dreams ⟜ Inspiring your happiness ⟜ Holding your hand and helping you through it all ⟜ In all of our days, our lives are always changing ⟜ Tears come along as well as smiles ⟜ Along the roads you travel, may the miles be a thousand times more lovely than lonely ⟜ May they give you gifts that never, ever end: someone wonderful to love and a dear friend in whom you can confide ⟜ May you have rainbows after every storm ⟜ May you have hopes to keep you safe and warm ⟜

⟜ And may you always have an angel
by your side ⟜

Every day, in the world around us, real-life angels are doing the things they do, bringing more smiles to the world around them.

Real-life angels build bridges instead of walls. They don't play hide-and-seek with the truth, and they don't have hidden agendas. They tend to be the only ones who understand what you're going through. If they sense that you're hurting, they do whatever they can to help you.

Real-life angels understand difficulties and always give the benefit of the doubt.

They don't hold others up to standards they can't live by themselves. Real-life angels are what "inner beauty" is all about.

They walk beside you when you could benefit from a little guidance and direction in your life. And they support you in your attempts to do what is right.

If you come across an angel like this, you are one of the luckiest people of all. If someone in your life is wonderfully like an angel to you, it's important to thank them for the blessing.

And may you be blessed
with everything
that could ever bring...
a smile to your life

*May you be blessed
with all these things...*

An abundance of happiness.
*Feelings that warm your world
and make you smile.*
*Friends and loved ones by your side...
people who are going to treasure every
memory they get to make with you.*

Wonderful surprises in your life.
Beautiful sunrises in your days.
Opportunities that come along.
Chances you've hoped for.

Goals you've been striving to reach.
Changes you've wanted to make.
A song in your heart.
A wish that comes true.

And reminders of how much nicer
this world is... all because of you.

About the Author

Best-selling author and editor Douglas Pagels has inspired millions of readers with his insights and his anthologies. His books have sold over 3 million copies, and he is one of the most-quoted contemporary writers on the Internet today. Reflecting a philosophy that is perfect for our times, Doug has a wonderful knack for sharing his thoughts and sentiments in a voice that is so positive and understanding we can't help but take the message to heart.

Visiting Mount Cook on New Zealand's South Island

His writings have been translated into over a dozen languages due to their global appeal and inspiring outlook on life, and his work has been quoted by many worthy causes and charitable organizations.

He and his wife live in Colorado, and they are the parents of children in college and beyond. Over the years, Doug has spent much of his time as a classroom volunteer, a youth basketball coach, an advocate for local environmental issues, a frequent traveler, and a craftsman, building a cabin in the Rocky Mountains.